YOUR KNOWLEDGE HAS VALUE

Junaid Javaid

Costs & Benefits of each Source of Capital

GRIN Verlag

Bibliografische Information der Deutschen Nationalbibliothek:

Die Deutsche Bibliothek verzeichnet diese Publikation in der Deutschen National-bibliografie; detaillierte bibliografische Daten sind im Internet über http://dnb.d-nb.de/ abrufbar.

Dieses Werk sowie alle darin enthaltenen einzelnen Beiträge und Abbildungen sind urheberrechtlich geschützt. Jede Verwertung, die nicht ausdrücklich vom Urheberrechtsschutz zugelassen ist, bedarf der vorherigen Zustimmung des Verla-ges. Das gilt insbesondere für Vervielfältigungen, Bearbeitungen, Übersetzungen, Mikroverfilmungen, Auswertungen durch Datenbanken und für die Einspeicherung und Verarbeitung in elektronische Systeme. Alle Rechte, auch die des auszugsweisen Nachdrucks, der fotomechanischen Wiedergabe (einschließlich Mikrokopie) sowie der Auswertung durch Datenbanken oder ähnliche Einrichtungen, vorbehalten.

Imprint:

Copyright © 2013 GRIN Verlag GmbH
Druck und Bindung: Books on Demand GmbH, Norderstedt Germany
ISBN: 978-3-656-74896-0

This book at GRIN:

http://www.grin.com/en/e-book/281115/costs-benefits-of-each-source-of-capital

GRIN - Your knowledge has value

Der GRIN Verlag publiziert seit 1998 wissenschaftliche Arbeiten von Studenten, Hochschullehrern und anderen Akademikern als eBook und gedrucktes Buch. Die Verlagswebsite www.grin.com ist die ideale Plattform zur Veröffentlichung von Hausarbeiten, Abschlussarbeiten, wissenschaftlichen Aufsätzen, Dissertationen und Fachbüchern.

Visit us on the internet:

http://www.grin.com/

http://www.facebook.com/grincom

http://www.twitter.com/grin_com

TASK-2: COST & BENEFITS OF EACH SOURCE OF CAPITAL

FINAL REPORT

BSS000-6: APPLIED MANAGEMENT PROJECT

WRITTEN & SUBMITTED BY:

JUNAID JAVAID

DATE OF SUBMISSION:

29/04/2013

TABLE OF CONTENTS

There are many cases have been observed where the shareholders' capital was not adequate enough to support the company's working capital requirement which matter a lot to the companies' growth and survival. Majority of time it has been observed and analysed that the companies considering to meet its working capital through the external sources are aware of every aspect of the different financial sources. It is important for the companies to take certain parameter (interest rate, term of usage, impact on company's financial leverage, conditions of lending agreement, time to get the lending approval and the impact of proposed source on the company's financial ratios) into consideration while making the financing decisions. The theory of Capital Structure is extensively be used to get insight that how much risky is the company's approach in using external sources (prominently debt). The Trade-off theory intended that companies must have to balance the costs and the benefits of debts flow within the enterprises. Different sources of capital can be classified in various manners but for the convenience, the all of these sources are classified in to following categories (Security Financing, Internal Financing, Loan Financing, Lease Financing and Other sources). Shanghai General Motors Corporation (SGMC) is regarded as the largest international joint venture undertook in China. This venture was made for the accomplishment of long-term goals established by the both firms' executive. The capital contributed by General Motors (GM)-China of $350 Million to the SGMC. $350 Million equivalent was contributed by SAIC to the SGMC. For meeting the working capital needs, SGMC required $821 Million Of which about the equivalent of $460 Million contributed through Chinese Banks and the Equivalent of of $361 Million was contributed through the International Banks. It has been understood that Different sources of capital have their positive and weak aspects to the associated companies. Therefore the company should use more than source of capital which thus would be resulted in forming company's efficient portfolio of financing. In this manner by capitalising on different sources of capital, the company would be able to leverage its risk level. And if the associated company is risk averse then it should go for Security Financing or Loan Financing.

CHAPTER-1: AIMS & OBJECTIVES

1.1. Background Context

The companies' business capital is regarded as the advanced source of finance for the meeting the working capital needs (Cooper, et al., 1994; Cressy, 2006). There are many cases have been observed where the shareholders' capital was not adequate enough to support the company's working capital requirement which matter a lot to the companies' growth and survival (Evans & Jovanovic, 1989). So in this situation they found the external source as a feasible option for them. Although these sources incorporates the cost which has to be paid by the borrowing company according the agreement signed at the initial stages and if the company tries to dodge the lenders then the lenders holds the authority in many cases to force the company go bankrupt. But on the other hand, the fund received by the company in the result of the lending agreement can support company in numerous ways, which not only intended the company to go through the development stages through the continuous expansion but also could enable the remain competitive in the long-run.

In the area of Corporate Finance, this process of acquiring funds from the different sources is known as the Financing Decision. Now a day, the Corporations are fiercely hiring the corporate managers for this particular process, because this process could permit the corporation to go through the projects which looks impossible for them to undergo on the individual basis. So this process not only resulted in maximizing the wealth of the company's shareholders but also give the incentive back to the investors for making that major investment and keeping the trust on the company. Although there are many theories which intended the companies to try its best to utilise the fund from its available resources in order to keep the dividend to be paid the companies' shareholders on the maximum level. One of that theory developed is Pecking Order Theory which alleged the company to look for its internal resources first at the time of making financial decision and if the company finds it really hard to meet the working capital requirement then it should verify the external resources. This theory is emphasised more on keeping the company's debt and equity side on the balance term, this fact not only keeps the company's financial position stagnant but also keeps the company to be focused more on towards the completion of its operations which is directly related to its corporate objective rather than diverted the company's intention towards controlling and solving its debt repayment problems.

But in real sense, it has been proved that the Debt is best alternative available at hand for the companies with good credit ratings. This source is also cheap and sometime resulted in enhancing the firm's enterprise value and also gives the company an option to pursue the projects which incorporates higher return for its stakeholders. The debt is the best source which increases the size of the given industry and thus keeping the entering barriers higher which then keeps the given industry attractive and more competitive.

There is also another set of studies which discussed the fact that the companies before making the financial decisions are going to evaluate the cost and benefit of each source. So this point drawn the fact majority of time the companies to meet its working capital through the external sources are aware of every consent of the different financial sources. And sometime it has also been observed that the companies are sourcing funds from multiple sources which not only intended the companies to expand its existing operations in rapid manner but also to decrease the cost of capital.

Another study has outlined certain parameter which must be taken into consideration while making the financing decisions. The first one is to carefully analysed the interest rate of each source of capital. The second one is term of usage of particular sources. The next point is related to consider the effect of each source of capital on its company's financial leverage. The next important point to settle the term of lending agreement on the initial stages so that it would not threaten the company in the future. The company also have to stimulate the effect of each source on the company's financial performance and also on its financial position as well. The company also has to analyse that how long each source would take to approve so as the company would able to meet its working capital needs on time.

1.2. Problem Statement

In order to meet the working capital requirements, the companies needed to identify and evaluate the cost and the benefits of each source of capital through which the companies would able to employ funds in the current operations. These all sources are needed to carefully evaluated which would enable the company to make the financial decision regarding its financial leverage in the effective and efficient manner.

1.3. Aims & Objectives

The main aim of this report is to inform the readers about the all possible sources of capital which would permit the company to meet its working capital needs in a wise manner. This report will include the advantages and disadvantages of each funding source from the different Scholars' perspectives. Hence this report will also include some case studies which will intended the company towards the successfully stories of number of organisation which were not only able to use the debts on the optimum level but also encompasses itself successfully from the stage of survival and expansion.

The central focus of this report is emphasised on the way of finding the appropriate source of finance which not only increases the company's capability to accomplish its strategic level objectives but also leaded the company to maximise its shareholders' wealth which is an important purpose of company's financial management. The academic research objectives behind this Applied Management Project are briefly discussed below:

- To learn about the different sources of capital which can be employed and utilised by the corporation the meet its working capital needs.
- To discover the distinct features of each source of capital, which make each source separable and unique from the other sources.
- To understand the importance of the financial decision making with the companies which usually covers the large proportion of its working capital needs from utilisation and harmonisation of these all sources.
- To evaluate the pros and cons of each source of capital with the intention of make a judgement that in what manner each specified source can support the

company in improving its financial position and also to have good impact of these sources on the company's financial performance over a long-run.

1.4. Summary

There are many cases have been observed where the shareholders' capital was not adequate enough to support the company's working capital requirement which matter a lot to the companies' growth and survival. The Pecking Order theory is emphasised more on keeping the company's debt and equity side on the balance term, this fact not only keeps the company's financial position stagnant but also keeps the company to be focused more on towards the completion of its operations which is directly related to its corporate objective rather than diverted the company's intention towards controlling and solving its debt repayment problems. The usage of debt is cheap and sometime resulted in enhancing the firm's enterprise value and also gives the company an option to pursue the projects which incorporates higher return for its stakeholders. Majority of time it has been observed and analysed that the companies considering to meet its working capital through the external sources are aware of every aspect of the different financial sources. It is important for the companies to take certain parameter (interest rate, term of usage, impact on company's financial leverage, conditions of lending agreement, time to get the lending approval and the impact of proposed source on the company's financial ratios) into consideration while making the financing decisions. The fundamental objective of this report is to suggest the corporation with the appropriate source of finance which not only increases the company's capability to accomplish its strategic level objectives but also leaded the company to maximise its shareholders' wealth which is an important purpose of company's financial management.

The next chapter will review the literature on the cost and benefit of each source of capital which are categorised on the basis of nature of financing which could be utilised to meet the working capital needs.

CHAPTER-2: LITERATURE REVIEW

2.1. Capital Structure

The matter of meeting the companies' working capital requirements is directly linked up with concept of Capital Structure (Modigliani & Miller, 1958). This concept analysed the company's capital composition in term of equity and debt employed in the company. Many Scholars are of perspective that the company's capital structure helps the outside evaluators to analyse the mixture of different sources of capital being utilised by the specified company in meeting its working capital needs (Dewatripont & Tirole, 1994). This concept is extensively be used to get insight that how much risky is the company's approach in using external sources (prominently debt). Normally the companies which are profoundly financed through the debt capital are poses greater risk and in other sense these companies are ranked higher on the leverage scale (Myers, 2001).

2.2. Agency Theory

This concept of agency theory is used comprehensively to explain the type of relationship exist between the principals (Shareholders) and agents (Management), hence this theory deal with the resolving of problem which exist in the given agency relationship (Jensen & Meckling, 1976).

The introduction of debt or the increase of debt in the company's given capital may give rise to the agency problem (Jensen, 1986). This happen because of the fact the increase of debt is directly linked up with increase of cost of capital which not only incremented the operating expenses but also decrease the company's retained earnings as well. The second cause of problem in the agency relationship is the wealth transformation this happen as a result of raising capital through the long-term debt, which meant that the increase will also incremented the company's financial leverage which thus be resulted in the wealth transfers between given sets of beneficiaries (Shareholders). This wealth transfer will be occurred from the capital beneficiaries (Shareholders) to the income beneficiaries (Lenders or the Supplier of Funds). Thus larger the increase of debt made by the management will be resulted in increasing the extend of transfer of wealth in the same pattern described before.

2.3. Trade-off Theory

This concept refers to the thought that in order to meet the working capital needs, the companies have to balance the costs and the benefits of debts flow within the enterprises and this can only be done through the usage of debt only up to the optimisation level (Kraus & Litzenberger, 1973). Any increase beyond that point will no further increases the marginal benefits of debt but only be resulted increasing the marginal cost that debt. So it has been understood that this concept urge the Corporations to use the debt only up to the optimisation level which entails to offset the costs of debt in relation to the benefits of debts (Modigliani & Miller, 1963).

2.4. Sources of Capital

Commonly, there are different sources of capital available for the companies to meet its working capital needs. These working capital requirements are not only critical for the new firms in supporting its survival but also for also existing companies in supporting their expansion stage even in the period their maturity as well. Currently variety of financing opportunities are available in the financial markets which not give an incentive to the investors but also offering funding support to the companies at the less rate of return. So in this manner, the companies are not only successful in meeting its working capital requirements but also able boost up its retained earnings up to the desirable level.

These sources of capital can be classified in various manners but for the convenience, the all of these sources are classified in to following categories (Security Financing, Internal Financing, Loan Financing, Lease Financing and Other sources).

2.4.1. Security Financing

It is considered as the traditional source of finance through which the companies are initiating towards the intention of meeting its working capital need (Lawton, 1996). It is also regarded as the alternative of Loan Financing because these sources are backed by giving the lenders the ownership stakes within the company (Barr, 2005). In these financing options, the lenders usually buy the share issued by the company in the initial period of time and thus authorised to get the dividend payment at the end of every financial period (normally on semi-annual basis). Different forms of this financing will be discussed below with their appropriate advantages and disadvantages to the companies.

2.4.1.1. Ordinary Shares

This is the most widely used financing instrument in almost all industries (Stoltz, 2007). The corporations are looking to raise the capital through the issuance of ordinary shares which not gives the ownership authority in the given but also granted the voting rights which can be exercised in the context of making and setting the company's strategic objectives and strategic decisions (Alexander, et al., 2007). The advantages and disadvantages of this source are listed below:

Advantages

- The payment of dividends is only made in the condition where the company has the surplus retained earnings. This is a plus sign for the company who are unable to post enough profit during the specified financial period.
- The company is eligible to not to make the repayment of capital collected from as a result of this source until it declare itself as solvent.
- The company can source as much funds as it desire through this source. But the management has to keep track of this financial leverage which may be resulted in giving rise to the agency problem or liquidation situation in engaging firm.
- The accessibility feature of this source intended the company to use this source as a suitable option to meet its working capital requirements or also to keep the shareholders' wealth on the increasing pattern.

Disadvantages

- In term of cost, this source is not a suitable option because of two factors (Advertisement and Subscription). Although these costs incurred at once only but sometime bearing that much cost would indulged the company in more financial difficulty from which it is really difficult to make recovery.

- The loss of control feature is also incorporated in this source, which only resulted in the wealth transfers from the capital beneficiaries (Shareholders) to the income beneficiaries (Lenders or the Supplier of Funds) but also distribute the right to making strategic decisions the capital beneficiaries to the income beneficiaries.
- Sometime this source would take longer to get fund approval because of necessary procedures to be followed to meet the working capital requirements.
- Because of the transfer of wealth feature this source incorporates more risk with itself in the context of financial leverage. And thus this factor more frequently leads the companies towards the phenomena of increasing cost of capital which would have a bad impact on the companies' expected rate of return on the long-term basis.

2.4.1.2. Preference Shares

This hybrid source of finance can be used by the companies to meet its working capital needs. It is regarded as the hybrid security because of its characteristics as it can be employed in the form of debt or equity depending entirely upon the companies' financial needs and also on its financial position (Chandra, 2008). The holders of these shares are entitled to get regular payments of dividends at the end of each financial period but they don't have any voting rights within company's decision making (Bhattacharyya, 2006). But they got preference in relation to the ordinary shareholder in the situation where the company go bankrupt make the repayment of principal amount of its all shareholders (Dornseifer, 2005). The advantages and disadvantages of preference shares are outlined in the portion below:

Advantages

- The preference shareholders are not authorised to force the company to declare itself solvent in the case where the company is unable to make regular payment of dividends to them.
- Because of its hybrid feature, it can be utilised by the companies to reduce its financial leverage which would make the companies' financial position impressive

in the financial market and also reduces the liquidation risk attached with the too much usage of debts.

- The superior feature of this source is that it would not intend the company to dilute its existing shareholders' control which would also reduce the risk of arising of agency problem within the enterprises.

Disadvantages

- Most frequently when it is used as an equity, it incurred more expense to the specified firms as in that case it will not be categorised as the tax deductible expense because it will only be dividable from the funds listed as net profit in the company's statement of performance.
- Despite of the fact that the preference shareholders would not forced the company to declare for the bankruptcy in the event of not getting the dividend payments on consistent basis but this thing would make a bad impact on the given company's credit reputation which would indulged the company in to the problems of raising funds in the future time period and would surely be resulted in increasing the company's cost of capital by too much extend.

2.4.2. Internal Financing

The concept of internal financing reflects the company's approach of plough back of company's earnings for the purpose of meeting company's working capital requirements or for its expansion as well. This source of capital is heavily capitalised in the SME's sectors but in the corporations this source is being utilised on the rare occasion as the company has to make the payment of dividends to its shareholders at the frequent interval so after making this payment and paying management salaries (Burton, 2009), the corporations are left with very few fund which could not make enough impact on the company's financial performance (Keown, 2003).

2.4.2.1. Retained Profit

This is considered as the amount of fund which the company holds in its account after paying off all liabilities (Bossert, 2008). The retained profit is the most secured form of capital as it does not incorporate any cost of capital but sometime forced the companies to scrap its shareholders dividend payment for the specified period which could the permitted the company in expanding its existing operations or to meet its working capital requirements (Mohapatra, 1999).

Advantages

- This source could assist companies with least credit ratings in meeting its financial needs and sometime also to enhance its credit reputation within the existing industry.
- It support companies in lessening the burden of debt which is directly related with the companies' survival and growth factors.
- It could make possible for the companies, the issuance of bonus in the form of accumulated profits.
- It could be outcome in increasing the company's share prices as the company is able to depict in the financial statement that it holds huge funds in its reserves.
- It could strengthen the corporation's capital formation or composition.

Disadvantages

- Sometime it could forced the companies to scrap its shareholders' dividend payments for the specified period which could make bad impact on the shareholders' morale.
- It could lead the company towards the situation of over capitalisation which could weaken the company's financial position.
- It could signifies bad impact on the financial markets as it shows that the specified company is not much interested in distributing the incentive to the shareholders who are deserved to get such reward rather than reinvested in the operations.
- It could be resulted in arising of dispute as it is considered as too much difficult for the company to meet its expenses with this source of capital.
- It could intend the company's shareholders to closely monitor its management to anticipate that either the raising of capital is being utilised for the company interest or the management is doing this for its own interest.

2.4.3.   Loan Financing

It is to be termed as the source of capital which permitted the company to borrow required amount of capital with the intention of paying it back in the future time period (Bakker & Levey, 2012). It is also be known as the secured method of financing, as at the extensive level it frequently backed by the company's asset which could be liquidated in the event of company's failure in making repayments on time (Berdiev, 2006).

2.4.3.1. Bank Loans

This source of capital is utilised for the purpose of acquiring fund which are sorted to be repaid in accordance with terms and conditions signed at the initial stages (Harry, 2009). Normally, the repayment schedule is depends entirely on three factors which are: amount of capital, duration and the rate of interest to be charged (Lou, 2001). There are many businesses who finds this source as a crucial component of their financial structure. And in fact this source is easily accessible for the growing and well-established businesses (Carlson & Fabozzi, 1992). The lenders (Banks) of this source usually took into consideration track record of company's profitability which depicts the company's capabilities in repaying the loan fund along with the interest (Brigham & Daves, 2009).

Advantages

- The company can raise funds through this source on the long-term basis.
- It is always be backed by some type of asset which could be secured option for the banks especially in the cases where the companies declared itself solvent.
- It is without the risk of transforming companies' ownership and control to the lender which is frequent practiced in case of equity financing.
- The interest rate which is to collected by the banks as the charges for providing this financial support is usually fixed at the initial which thus be resulted in making easy for the companies to do projections.

Disadvantages

- Major drawback of this source from the company perspective is the security which would be pledged as an asset by the bank. In this context, bank becomes the company's creditor which holds the collateral on the specified asset and if there would be a case the company fails to repay the loan then the bank would have first call on that asset which could enable bank to recover its loss.
- This second negative aspect of this source lie in shape of lack of flexibility factor as the banks are always seems rigid in negotiating the interest rate which must be charged by the authority as the mean of their compensation and reward.

2.4.3.2. Debentures

The companies can use this source of finance for meetings its working capital needs (Hanif, 2001). The issuing of debentures is reliant on two factors which are: Rate of Interest and its Denomination (Kumar & Sharma, 2006). Debentures are used as debt instrument for financing long term needs (Rachchh, 2010). Although Debentures are considered as the risky source but it cost relatively less than the other sources (Ahmed, 2007).

Advantages

- This source of capital incorporate less cost as the interest payments to be made under this contract is tax deductible which could be resulted in decreasing operating expenses of the company.
- The absence of risks like dilution of shareholders' ownership & control makes this source favourable for the company's who are risk averse and always intended to go secured financing options.
- Utilisation of this source in a effective manner would permit the company to observe the loss of monetary outgo in the event of increasing of prices.

Disadvantages

- The companies who went for this source of capital are bounded to make interest payment at the frequent interval as it does not takes into consideration the economic condition of the company.

- If it is used in the form of debt financing then the companies have to repay the principal amount at the end of time period which could cause problem if the company would fall far below the financial projection.

2.4.4. Lease Financing

This form of sourcing is utilised in the form of agreement which is made between the company and lending firm for purpose of using given asset for the certain time period. In the proposed agreement, the lender of the Asset is called as Lessor and the user of that asset is known as Lessee (Biswasroy & Mishra, 1992). This contract will be beneficial for both parties. Lessor will able to get the rent of using specified asset at the regular interval whereas the Lessee will able to use the asset without having to make payment of lump sum at the initial stages (Nevitt & Fabozzi, 2000). This form of capital source can be divided into two types (Operating & Finance Lease), which are discussed in depth below portion.

2.4.4.1. Operating Lease

The lease is termed as Operating Lease, if the contract is made on the basis where the risk of ownership and control always remained at the Lessor side and the Lessee is only authorised to use the asset up to the expiration of contract and is bound to return the asset back to the Lessee (Khan, 2004). This lease type is also called as callable lease which can be cancelled at any time of the contract but must be made through the mutual consent of both parties (Walter, 2004). This lease form is eligible for the companies which are engaging in the industry where the asset become obsolete after the short interval of time (Besley & Brigham, 2008). The implication of this lease is heavily observed in the Airline industry.

2.4.4.2. Finance Lease

This lease contract is also called as Capital Lease which entails the features of transforming the risk of ownership and control to the Lessee at the end of the lease term (Burrell, et al., 1984). The Lessor is only authorised to get the lease payment to be made at regular interval up to the expiration of contract and after this agreement the Lessor is always bounded to give the ownership authority to the Lessee (Khan, 2008).

This form of lease is extensively capitalised with the central focus of Capital Outlay's Amortisation (Khan & Jain, 2006).

Advantages

- The companies would be able to use the underlying asset for the specific period of time without having to bear the fixed cost of asset's acquisition and also to capitalise the proposed fund for the financing of profitable projects.
- It could not make an impact on the company's financial leverage as it only accounted as expense on the company's financial statement.
- It would also provide the company with the protection shield especially in the industry where the asset becomes obsolete after a short span of time.
- It does not required any form of Declaration Norms regarding debt or equity at the time of signing the lease contract.

Disadvantages

- The Lessee cannot use the acquired asset for the purpose of getting Loan from the bank.
- In case of not making lease payment, the Lessor holds the authority to cancel the contract and bring back its leased asset as the Lessee violates the lease terms and conditions. So, it shows that it is not a good option for the companies with inconsistent financial performance.

2.4.5.   Other Source of Capital

2.4.5.1. Trade Credit

This financing source equipped the specified company with the option of procuring goods from supplier without having to make payment in advance (Gallagher & Andrew, 2008). The payment is normally made after the sale of specified goods. This type of facility is made available for the company once it has been assessed that the company's financial health sufficient enough to make payment of accrued credit (Blasio, 2003). Certain features (Flexibility & Ease of Accessibility) of this source made it as the prominent option for the company to get the advantage of.

Advantages

- It can be termed as the continuous financing source as it permitted the company to sell the products to be procured from the supplier first and then make payment of trade credit.
- Sourcing capital from this source may results in enhancing the specified company cash flow. As the company is allowed to make the payment of accrued credit after some interval of time which could be resulted in making the intensity of cash inflow more than the case outflow which thus intended the company to hold more fund in its disposal account which would be utilised in improving the enterprise's other operations.
- This could enable the company to get cash discount from the supplier. And it has been analysed that the companies are utilising this source at large level for the purpose of absorbing of additional cost in the event of decreasing the demand of the product procured from the particular supplier.

Disadvantages

- The bad point of this source is that it is directly linked with company's ability of making payment of accruals on the company in the given time frame. In case of not making payment on time could make huge impact on the company's credit reputation which could be resulted in weakening the company's buying power in term of credit basis.
- It could indulged given company in more problems especially in the cases where the company is unable to sell the products. So, if the contract does not included any refund option then the company needed to find another source in making payment of these accrued credits.

2.4.5.2. Venture Capital

This source of financing is usually used for sourcing project which incorporates greater risk of failure or success and if it work according to plan (Brian, 2000), it would permitted the investor as well as entrepreneur to generate abnormal rate of return (Gregoriou, et al., 2011). This contract entails one party to capitalise his/her experience and skills by the using the funds provided by another party (Caselli, 2009). The profit ratio is occasionally settled at the initial stages but in most cases the funding parties holds the right of getting more proportion (Ramsinghani, 2011). This source of capital is beneficial for the entrepreneur as they would not be bounded to contribute fund in case that the project does not go according to the desired projections (Landström & Mason, 2012).

Advantages

- It makes possible for the company with few funds to undergo a project which seems impossible for them to go through on the individual basis. And in the case of successful execution of proposed plan, it could create potential for them to source fund from other sources as well.
- It permits the investing party to gain benefits of enjoying abnormal rate of return and also after recovering the invested fund, invest the surplus fund in order projects with the intention of growing profit on the continuous basis.

Disadvantages

- In case of unfavourable condition, it would be the obligation on the investor to bear the loss rather than reclaiming fund from the entrepreneur who was only accountable for making his/her idea a practical implication.
- In case of successful execution, the entrepreneur would own very few proportion of ownership stakes as the major risk was contributed by other party who were solely responsible for bearing loss as well.

2.4.5.3. Overdraft

This source is regarded as the short-term source of capital and is provided as a facility by the banks to the companies to withdrawn more cash than the available balance existed in their accounts (Leonard, 2010). The banks normally charged nominal fees for using this facility and also put limit on the amount which could be overdrawn (Coyle, 2002). This facility is useful for the companies who have regular buying and selling in their account and without this facility it could leave the account with bad cash-flow condition (Nieman & Pretorius, 2004). It could proved to be a backup for the companies especially they have accrual credit to pay before receiving their invoice payment (Sofat & Hiro, 2010).

Advantages

- It is an useful option to be capitalised especially in the circumstances when the company runs out of cash and have liability to pay before the time of recovering funds from its customers. It thus help the companies in chasing their own payments and also supports in maintaining cash-flow.
- It is very easy for the companies to avail and thus proved to be smart cash-flow backup with lease objection.

Disadvantages

- This source cost more than the regular bank loans as the bank does not have any backup for providing this associated facility. It cost huge amount of money if the company withdrawn the cash more than the agreed overdraft limit.
- Banks are authorised to recall this facility at any course of time. But on the frequent basis, it happened when the companies are unable to repay the accrued amount or if the company has broken the terms and conditions of given facility,
- Sometime it may required the company to secure any business asset for availing this facility then in that case the company could be on the risk of losing the given asset in case of not making the repayment.

2.5. Summary

The theory of Capital Structure is extensively be used to get insight that how much risky is the company's approach in using external sources (prominently debt). Normally the companies which are profoundly financed through the debt capital are poses greater risk and in other sense these companies are ranked higher on the leverage scale. The increase of debt in the company's given capital may give rise to the agency, this happened because of the fact the increase of debt is directly linked up with increase of cost of capital which not only incremented the operating expenses but also decrease the company's retained earnings and sometime happened in form of wealth transformation from shareholders to its creditors in case of not paying debt. The Trade-off intended that companies must have to balance the costs and the benefits of debts flow within the enterprises and this can only be done through the usage of debt only up to the optimisation level. sources of capital can be classified in various manners but for the convenience, the all of these sources are classified in to following categories (Security Financing, Internal Financing, Loan Financing, Lease Financing and Other sources). Ordinary Shares are the most widely used financing instrument in almost all industries. Preference shares regarded as the hybrid security because of its characteristics as it can be employed in the form of debt or equity depending entirely upon the companies' financial needs and also on its financial position. The retained profit is the most secured form of capital as it does not incorporate any cost of capital but sometime forced the companies to scrap its shareholders dividend payment for the specified period. There are many businesses who find Bank Loans as a crucial component of their financial structure. And in fact this source is easily accessible for the growing and well-established businesses. Debentures are considered as the risky source of capital but it cost relatively less than the other sources. Lease contract will be beneficial for both parties. Lessor will able to get the rent of using specified asset at the regular interval whereas the Lessee will able to use the asset without having to make payment of lump sum at the initial stages. This facility of Trade Credit is made available for the company once it has been assessed that the company's financial health sufficient enough to make payment of accrued credit. The Venture Capital contract entails one party to capitalise his/her experience and skills by the using the funds provided by another party. The Overdraft facility is useful for the companies who have regular buying and selling in their account and without this facility it could leave the account with bad cash-flow condition. It could proved to be a backup for the companies especially they have accrual credit to pay before receiving their invoice payment.

The next chapter will contain the case study which shows the practical implication of capitalisation of different sources of finance in order to meet the working capital needs.

CHAPTER-3: CASE STUDY

1.1. Sources of Capital: A Case Study Of Shanghai General Motors Corporation (Nam, 2010)

Shanghai General Motors Corporation is regarded as the largest international joint venture undertook in China. This venture is actually a link between the World largest company (General Motors) and the Shanghai Automotive Industrial Corporation (SAIC). This venture was made for the accomplishment of long-term goals established by the both firms' executive. The SAIC was in the need of design and manufacturing expertise which could enabled them to acquire new customer base in the Chinese marketplace, whereas the GM (General Motors) wanted its presence in the Chinese market which could enabled them to accomplish the long objective to remain the Dominant Automobiles manufacture around the world. In order to accomplish each other objectives, these companies had decided to form alliance with the name of Shanghai General Motors Corporation (SGMC).

1.1.1. Capital Sources Capitalised for Shanghai General Motors Corporation (SGMC)

Capital Requirement for the start-up of automobile manufacturing is very high. The project of SGMC includes the facilities of manufacturing transmissions, engines and vehicles and thus regarded as expensive and complex facilities. Capital expenditures for fixed assets (automation, local infrastructure and equipment) for that proposed venture exceeded the amount of $1 Billion. As land could not be bought by companies in China so these requirements were meet through land granted from the Chinese government for the period of about 50 years. Capital inserted by both companies' shareholders is named as Registered Capital. This Registered Capital for SGMC amounted around $700 Million from GM & SAIC. The description of each source of capital is summarised in the below portion.

1.1.1.1. General Motors

The capital contributed by General Motors (GM)-China of $350 Million to the SGMC. GM-China is entirely owned as the subsidiary of General Motor Corporation.

1.1.1.2. Shanghai Automotive Industrial Corporation (SAIC)

$350 Million equivalent was contributed by SAIC to the SGMC. These funds gathered through two sources: Shanghai Automotive Industrial Corporation (SAIC) & Shanghai Automotive Joint Stock Company (SAJSC). SAIC was managed to acquired the fund of $217 Million which accounts for 62% percent of SAIC total assets and the remaining $133 Million was contributed through SAJSC which is a subsidiary of SAIC but is publicly owned on the partial basis via stock sales. However due to the specified restrictions imposed by Chinese Stock Exchanges the funding to SGMC through this source of capital is no longer available.

1.1.1.3. Working Capital Needs

The proposed venture required the approval from the Chinese central government which were applied through the process known as Registration Process. So, the Registration of given Joint Venture and the Initial Capital were done by both companies' shareholders which is called as Equity Financing. But there were more capital to be needed which comes beyond the initial capital is the working capital needs which includes the included the buying of certain machinery and equipments. So for meeting the working capital needs, SGMC required $821 Million which were contributed through the loan package termed as Debt Financing, the key information of that loan package is given below:

- There were almost 39 Chinese and International Bank who contributed in the loan package designed for SGMC.
- Of which about the equivalent of $460 Million (which accounted for 56% of Loan Packages) was contributed through the Chinese Banks.
- And the Equivalent of of $361 Million (which accounted for almost 44% of Loan Packages) was contributed through the International Banks operating in Hong Kong, Shanghai and in other Asian countries.

The whole summary of what was explained above is depicted in the figure below:

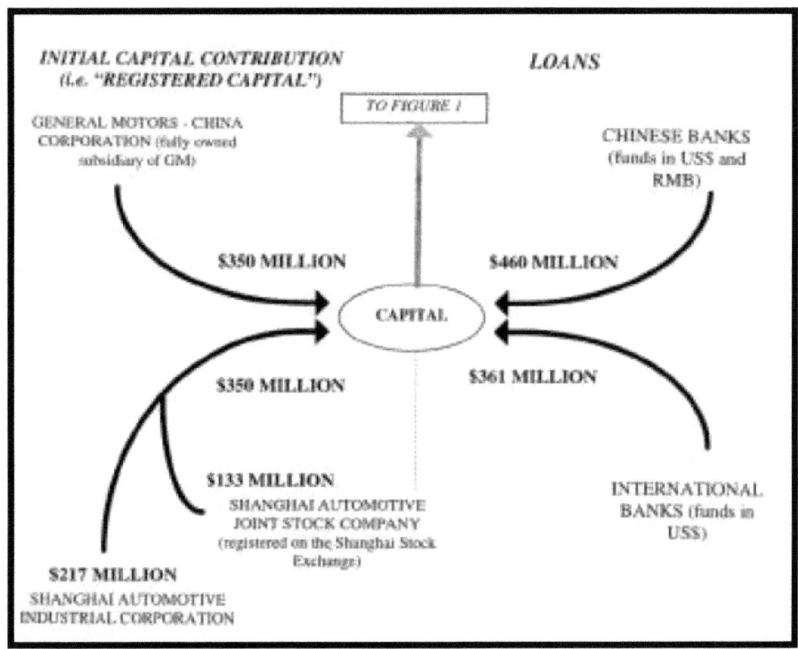

FIGURE 1 CAPITAL SOURCES FOR SHANGHAI GENERAL MOTORS CORPORATION, ADOPTED FROM (MURRAY, 2005)

It is important to outline here that the scope, visibility and scale of this international Joint Venture project are resulted in making the capital procurement procedure for Shanghai General Motors Corporation anomalous. Few Factors which contributed to the success of proposed capital arrangement was the 39 Banks' Consortium which involved the size and leverage applied by General Motors Treasury Office with the major banking partners (Bank of America, Deutsche Bank, Citicorp and others).

1.1.1.4. Findings

Currently in Chinese Business Environment, certain opportunities which could be capitalised in raising capital without banks is limited especially for the companies which are to be funded through foreign companies. Moreover the use of bonds for raising long term debt is made restricted through the complex procedures which also include government approval. And because of so many restrictions, in many cases it have been observed that long-term loan for International Joint Venture is conducted through the International Banks operating in China. But the debt to be raised meeting working capital requirement for the Sino-Foreign Joint Ventures is conducted through the combination of Chinese and International Banks. And the focus of foreign companies to raise capital through foreign capital sources emphasised mostly on two objectives: 1) to preserve capital resources for local firms and 2) enhancing capital inflow within the Chinese economy. So, it has been understood that the size and influence of SGMC permitted both companies (GM & SAIC) to overcome the obstacles imposed by the Chinese bureaucracy on the foreign companies to operate in China.

1.2. Summary

Shanghai General Motors Corporation is regarded as the largest international joint venture undertook in China. This venture was made for the accomplishment of long-term goals established by the both firms' executive. The SAIC was in the need of design and manufacturing expertise which could enabled them to acquire new customer base in the Chinese marketplace, whereas the GM (General Motors) wanted its presence in the Chinese market which could enabled them to accomplish the long objective to remain the Dominant Automobiles manufacture around the world. The project of SGMC includes the facilities of manufacturing transmissions, engines and vehicles and thus regarded as expensive and complex facilities. The capital contributed by General Motors (GM)-China of $350 Million to the SGMC. $350 Million equivalent was contributed by SAIC to the SGMC. These funds gathered. For meeting the working capital needs, SGMC required $821 Million which were contributed through the loan package termed as Debt Financing. There were almost 39 Chinese and International Bank who contributed in the loan package designed for SGMC. Of which about the equivalent of $460 Million (which accounted for 56% of Loan Packages) was contributed through the Chinese Banks. And the Equivalent of of $361 Million (which accounted for almost 44% of Loan Packages) was contributed through the International Banks operating in Hong Kong, Shanghai and in other Asian countries. The scope, visibility and scale of this international Joint Venture project were resulted in making the capital procurement procedure for Shanghai General Motors Corporation anomalous.

CHAPTER-4: DISCUSSION & CONCLUSION

4.1. Discussion

Security Financing is considered to be a primary option for the listed company. Its certain characteristics like low cost and quick way of fund acquisition makes it a prominent option for the associated companies. The other benefits of availing the financial institution services for the proposed purpose would be resulted in strengthening issuing companies' confidence level. Aside from the positive aspects of Security Financing are the aspects of company's effort to go through restricted regulatory demands and public scrutiny which could be resulted in reducing the company's independence in term of making decisions. So it reflected that the specified company should needed to acquire ethical considerations as the indirect mean of using unlimited public capital. Internal Financing in the form of Retained profit is also regarded as good policy pursued by the listed firms by delaying the payment of dividends to be made to the shareholders. This option is useful when the company is undergoing the stages of initial start-up or expansion. But pursuing of this policy at the maturity stage could be resulted in disrupting the shareholders' loyalty with the given company. From the perspective of listed companies the retained profit is considered as the strategic source of capital as it is to be utilised to finance new projects. It has been capitalised as the source of finance because it would not be resulted in the loss of control from the given shareholders. It is to be ascertain that the fund utilised from this source would permitted the company to finance new project on the solely basis. Loan Financing is also considered as easily accessible source for raising long term capital but certain things resulted in making it as least preferable source. In the event of not making repayment may affect the companies' credit reputation and also could indulged the given company in severe situation especially from the perspective of raising fund from any other sources. And in the circumstances of companies having bad revenue and projected return would restrict the company in the task of paying more interest than the normal market interest rate. So, in general it has been drawn that the ease of capitalising the loan financing option resulted in offsetting the risk of default. Leasing Financing is a good mean of acquiring and allocating expensive machinery and equipments. This would permitted the companies to layout funds and they also does not needed to remain conscious about the maintenance to be done on the frequent basis. Finance Lease would also allowed transferring the ownership of leased assets to the Lessee at the end of lease contract. Venture Capital is a good way which denominates the potential of flattering profitable from the future perspective of venture capitalists. It could thus create support by lender of funds (wealthy investors), it enable the companies who cannot afford certain projects to pursue them in an effort to build-up profitable venture in the short span of time. The core objective of this source of capital is the kind of generous support from the wealthy investors to the prospective firms. In relation to the financial support provided by the financial institutions, Venture Capital could extend its financing to projects which incorporates high risk with minimal guarantee of providing return more than the available market return. The bottleneck of this financing source is that it involves huge possibility that the management of prospective firm would lose its control over the governance. Venture Capital also included the distribution of profits where the major proportion is to be taken by the funding firm. Trade Credit is useful source for meeting working capital requirements as in business it's common practice to buy goods and to pay for them on the later stages. The company's supplier usually sends a statement (containing the information that how much credit is owned) at the end of each month. The company then has to give them the time frame in between it must need to make payment. So from this AMP, it has been understood that Different sources of capital have their positive and weak aspects to the associated companies. Therefore the company should use more than source of capital which thus would be resulted in forming company's efficient portfolio of financing. To prove this particular point, imagine that the company's perceived that it would lose its ownership control if continues to issue shares for raising long-term funds so it can off-set this risk by stop the issuing and starting to buy back the shares. Whereas, the more financing need would be sourced through the bank loans. And in this manner by capitalising different sources of capital the company would be able to leverage its risk level. And if the associated company is risk averse then it should go for Security or Loan Financing. In general the company has plenty of options to be undertaken to get support during the turbulent times.

4.2. Conclusion

There are many cases have been observed where the shareholders' capital was not adequate enough to support the company's working capital requirement which matter a lot to the companies' growth and survival. The Pecking Order theory is emphasised more on keeping the company's debt and equity side on the balance term, this fact not only keeps the company's financial position stagnant but also keeps the company to be focused more on towards the completion of its operations which is directly related to its corporate objective rather than diverted the company's intention towards controlling and solving its debt repayment problems. The usage of debt is cheap and sometime resulted in enhancing the firm's enterprise value and also gives the company an option to pursue the projects which incorporates higher return for its stakeholders. Majority of time it has been observed and analysed that the companies considering to meet its working capital through the external sources are aware of every aspect of the different financial sources. It is important for the companies to take certain parameter (interest rate, term of usage, impact on company's financial leverage, conditions of lending agreement, time to get the lending approval and the impact of proposed source on the company's financial ratios) into consideration while making the financing decisions. The fundamental objective of this report is to suggest the corporation with the appropriate source of finance which not only increases the company's capability to accomplish its strategic level objectives but also leaded the company to maximise its shareholders' wealth which is an important purpose of company's financial management.

The theory of Capital Structure is extensively be used to get insight that how much risky is the company's approach in using external sources (prominently debt). Normally the companies which are profoundly financed through the debt capital are poses greater risk and in other sense these companies are ranked higher on the leverage scale. The increase of debt in the company's given capital may give rise to the agency, this happened because of the fact the increase of debt is directly linked up with increase of cost of capital which not only incremented the operating expenses but also decrease the company's retained earnings and sometime happened in form of wealth transformation from shareholders to its creditors in case of not paying debt. The Trade-off intended that companies must have to balance the costs and the benefits of debts flow within the enterprises and this can only be done through the usage of debt only up to the optimisation level. sources of capital can be classified in various manners but for the convenience, the all of these sources are classified in to following categories (Security Financing, Internal Financing, Loan Financing, Lease Financing and Other sources). Ordinary Shares are the most widely used financing instrument in almost all industries. Preference shares regarded as the hybrid security because of its characteristics as it can be employed in the form of debt or equity depending entirely upon the companies' financial needs and also on its financial position. The retained profit is the most secured form of capital as it does not incorporate any cost of capital but sometime forced the companies to scrap its shareholders dividend payment for the specified period. There are many businesses who find Bank Loans as a crucial component of their financial structure. And in fact this source is easily accessible for the growing and well-established businesses. Debentures are considered as the risky source of capital but it cost relatively less than the other sources. Lease contract will be beneficial for both parties. Lessor will able to get the rent of using specified asset at the regular interval whereas the Lessee will able to use the asset without having to make payment of lump sum at the initial stages. This facility of Trade Credit is made available for the company once it has been assessed that the company's financial health sufficient enough to make payment of accrued credit. The Venture Capital contract entails one party to capitalise his/her experience and skills by the using the funds provided by another party. The Overdraft facility is useful for the companies who have regular buying and selling in their account and without this facility it could leave the account with bad cash-flow condition. It could proved to be a backup for the companies especially they have accrual credit to pay before receiving their invoice payment.

Shanghai General Motors Corporation is regarded as the largest international joint venture undertook in China. This venture was made for the accomplishment of long-term goals established by the both firms' executive. The SAIC was in the need of design and manufacturing expertise which could enabled them to acquire new customer base in the Chinese marketplace, whereas the GM (General Motors) wanted its presence in the Chinese market which could enabled them to accomplish the long objective to remain the Dominant Automobiles manufacture around the world. The project of SGMC includes the facilities of manufacturing transmissions, engines and vehicles and thus regarded as expensive and complex facilities. The capital contributed by General Motors (GM)-China of $350 Million to the SGMC. $350 Million equivalent was contributed by SAIC to the SGMC. These funds gathered. For meeting the working capital needs, SGMC required $821 Million which were contributed through the loan package termed as Debt Financing. There were almost 39 Chinese and International Bank who contributed in the loan package designed for SGMC. Of which about the equivalent of $460 Million (which accounted for 56% of Loan Packages) was contributed through the Chinese Banks. And the Equivalent of of $361 Million (which accounted for almost 44% of Loan Packages) was contributed through the International Banks operating in Hong Kong, Shanghai and in other Asian countries. The scope, visibility and scale of this international Joint Venture project were resulted in making the capital procurement procedure for Shanghai General Motors Corporation anomalous. The other factor which contributed to the success of proposed capital arrangement was the 39 Banks' Consortium.

4.3. Recommendation

it has been understood that Different sources of capital have their positive and weak aspects to the associated companies. Therefore the company should use more than source of capital which thus would be resulted in forming company's efficient portfolio of financing. In this manner by capitalising on different sources of capital, the company would be able to leverage its risk level. And if the associated company is risk averse then it should go for Security Financing or Loan Financing. In general the company has plenty of options to be undertaken to get support during the turbulent times.

CHAPTER-5: REFERENCES

Ahmed, N., 2007. *Corporate Accounting.* New Delhi: Atlantic Publishers & Dist.

Alexander, D., Britton, A. & Jorissen, A., 2007. *International Financial Reporting and Analysis.* 3rd ed. Mason: Cengage Learning EMEA.

Bakker, A. & Levey, M. M., 2012. *Transfer Pricing and Intra-group Financing: The Entangled Worlds of Financial Markets and Transfer Pricing.* Amsterdam: IBFD (International Bureau of Fiscal Documentation).

Barr, N. A., 2005. *Financing Higher Education: Answers From The Uk.* London: Routledge.

Berdiev, N., 2006. *Loan Financing Guide for Small Business Owners.* New York: Small Business Empowerment Pub.

Besley, S. & Brigham, E. F., 2008. *Essentials of managerial finance.* 14th ed. Mason: Cengage Learning.

Bhattacharyya, 2006. *Financial Accounting For Business Managers.* 3rd ed. New Delhi: PHI Learning Pvt. Ltd.

Biswasroy, P. K. & Mishra, D. P., 1992. *Lease Financing In India.* Mumbai: Kanishka Publishers.

Blasio, G. D., 2003. *Does Trade Credit Substitute Bank Credit? Evidence from Firm-level Data.* Washington: International Monetary Fund.

Bossert, T., 2008. *Methods of Equity Financing.* Norderstedt: GRIN Verlag.

Brian, C., 2000. *Venture Capital and Buyouts.* Chicago: Global Professional Publishi.

Brigham, E. F. & Daves, P. R., 2009. *Intermediate Financial Management (Book Only).* 10th ed. Mason: Cengage Learning.

Burrell, C. T., Marsden, E. & Petrie, J. C., 1984. *Lease Financing, Finance Company Lease Agreements: Papers.* Tronto: Queensland Law Society Incorporated.

Burton, M., 2009. *The financial system and the economy: principles of money and banking.* 5th ed. New York: M.E. Sharpe.

Carlson, J. H. & Fabozzi, F. J., 1992. *The Trading and securitization of senior bank loans.* Michigan: Probus Pub. Co.

Caselli, S., 2009. *Private Equity and Venture Capital in Europe: Markets, Techniques, and Deals.* London: Academic Press.

Chandra, 2008. *Financial Management: CFM-McGraw-Hill professional series in finance.* 7th ed. New Delhi: Tata McGraw-Hill Education.

Coyle, B., 2002. *Bank Finance: Debt and Equity Markets.* Kent: Global Professional Publishi.

Dewatripont, M. & Tirole, J., 1994. A Theory of Debt and Equity: Diversity of Securities and Manager-Shareholder Congruence. *The Quarterly Journal of Economics,* 109(4), pp. 1027-1054.

Dornseifer, F., 2005. *Corporate Business Forms in Europe: A Compendium of Public And Private Limited Companies in Europe.* Munchen: sellier. european law publ.

Evans, D. & Jovanovic, B., 1989. An Estimated Model of Entrepreneurial Choice Under Liquidity Constraints. *The Journal of Political Economy,* 97(4), p. 808.

Gallagher & Andrew, 2008. *Financial Management; Principles and Practice.* New York: Freeload Press, Inc..

Gregoriou, G. N., Kooli, M. & Kraeussl, R., 2011. *Venture Capital in Europe.* Oxford: Butterworth-Heinemann.

Hanif, M., 2001. *Volume 1 of Modern Accountancy, Modern Accountancy.* 2nd ed. New Delhi: Tata McGraw-Hill Education.

Harry, H., 2009. *Bank Loans and Stock Exchange Speculation.* Reprint ed. Amsterdam: BiblioBazaar.

Jensen, M. C. .., 1986. Agency Costs of Free Cash Flow, Corporate Finance, and Takeovers.. *American Economic Review,* 76(2), p. 323.

Jensen, M. C. & Meckling, W., 1976. JenTheory of the Firm: Managerial Behavior, Agency Costs and Ownership Structure. , 3(4): 305-360.. *Journal of Financial Economics,* 3(4), pp. 305-360.

Keown, A. J., 2003. *Foundations of Finance: The Logic and Practice of Financial Management.* 4th ed. Hong Kong: Reprint.

Khan & Jain, 2006. *Mafa Ca Final.* 2nd ed. New Delhi: Tata McGraw-Hill Education.

Khan, M. Y., 2004. *Financial Management: Text, Problems And Cases.* 2nd ed. New Delhi: Tata McGraw-Hill Education.

Khan, M. Y., 2008. *Cost Acctg N Fin Mgmt 4 Ca Pcc.* 3rd ed. New Delhi: Tata McGraw-Hill Education.

Kraus, A. & Litzenberger, R., 1973. A State-Preference Model of Optimal Financial Leverage. *Journal of Finance,* 28(4), pp. 911-922.

Kumar, R. & Sharma, V., 2006. *Auditing: Principles and Practice.* New Delhi: PHI Learning Pvt. Ltd.

Landström, H. & Mason, C. M., 2012. *Handbook of Research on Venture Capital.* 2nd ed. Northampton: Edward Elgar Publishing.

Lawton, S. B., 1996. *Financing Canadian Education,* Tronto: Canadian Education Association.

Leonard, B., 2010. *Study of Bank Overdraft Programs.* Chicago: DIANE Publishing.

Lou, J., 2001. *China's troubled bank loans: workout and prevention.* California: Kluwer Academic Publishers.

Modigliani, F. & Miller, M., 1958. The Cost of Capital, Corporation Finance and the Theory of Investment. , 48(3): 261.. *American Economic Review,* 48(3), p. 261.

Modigliani, F. & Miller, M., 1963. *Corporate Income Taxes and the Cost of Capital: A Correction. American Economic Association..* [Online]
Available at:
http://search.ebscohost.com/login.aspx?direct=true&db=buh&AN=8743472&site=ehost-live
[Accessed 03 March 2013].

Mohapatra, A. D., 1999. *Corporate Financial Management.* New Delhi: Discovery Publishing House.

Murray, M. J., 2005. *SOURCES OF CAPITAL FOR A SINO-FOREIGN EQUITY JOINT VENTURE: A CASE STUDY OF SHANGHAI GENERAL MOTORS CORPORATION,* Knoxville: Tennessee State University.

Myers, S., 2001. Capital Structure. *Journal of Economic Perspectives,* 15(2), pp. 81-102.

Nam, K.-M., 2010. *Learning through the International Joint Venture: Lessons from the Experience of China's Automotive Sector,* Beijing: Working Paper Series.

Nevitt, P. K. & Fabozzi, F. J., 2000. *Project Financing.* 7th ed. London: Euromoney Books.

Nieman, G. & Pretorius, M., 2004. *Managing Growth: A Guide for Entrepreneurs.* Cape Town: Juta and Company Ltd.

Rachchh, M. A., 2010. *Financial Accounting.* New Delhi: Pearson Education India.

Ramsinghani, M., 2011. *The Business of Venture Capital: Insights from Leading Practitioners on the Art of Raising a Fund, Deal Structuring, Value Creation, and Exit Strategies.* San Francisco: John Wiley & Sons.

Sofat, R. & Hiro, P., 2010. *Basic Accounting.* 2nd ed. New Delhi: PHI Learning Pvt. Ltd.

Stoltz, A., 2007. *financial management.* Cape Town: Pearson South Africa.

Walter, R. W., 2004. *Financing Your Small Business.* New York: Barron's Educational Series.